AF230956

THAT'S EASY

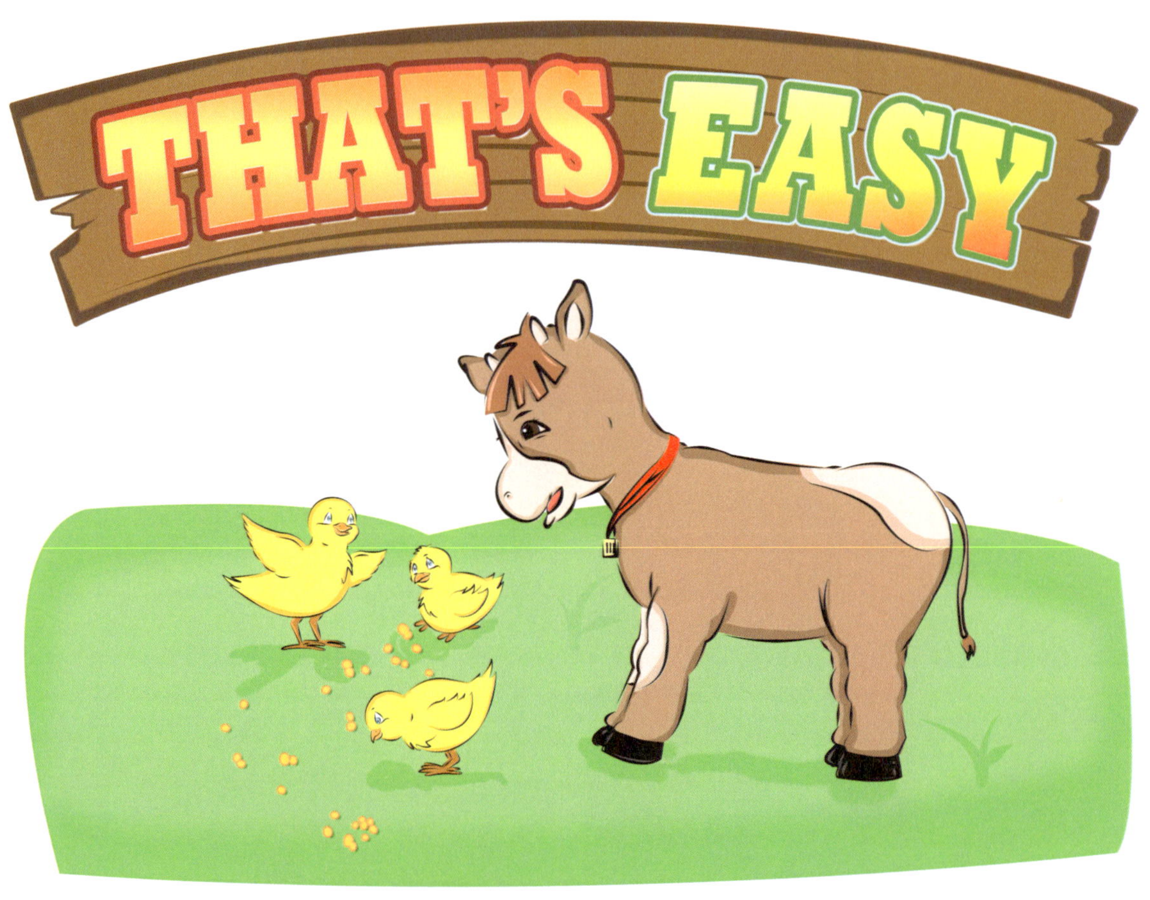

WRITTEN BY **JASON JONES** & ILLUSTRATED BY **SHERI JOSEPH**

For information to reproduce selections from this book, visit

www.thatseasybook.com

Library of Congress Cataloging-in-Publication-Data

Jason Jones

That's Easy / Jason Jones

Summary: That's Easy is a story that demonstrates how our different talents make us a unique creation from God A small baby cow tries to do things that the other animals can do. He discovers what is easy for them is not alwa for others. Admiration from the other animals leads the discovery of what is Easy for him.

Written by Jason Jones
Illustrated by Sheri Joseph in pen and paper & digital media

ISBN 978-1-944786-76-2 (ePDF)

It was the first day of spring, and all the baby animals came out to play for the very first time.

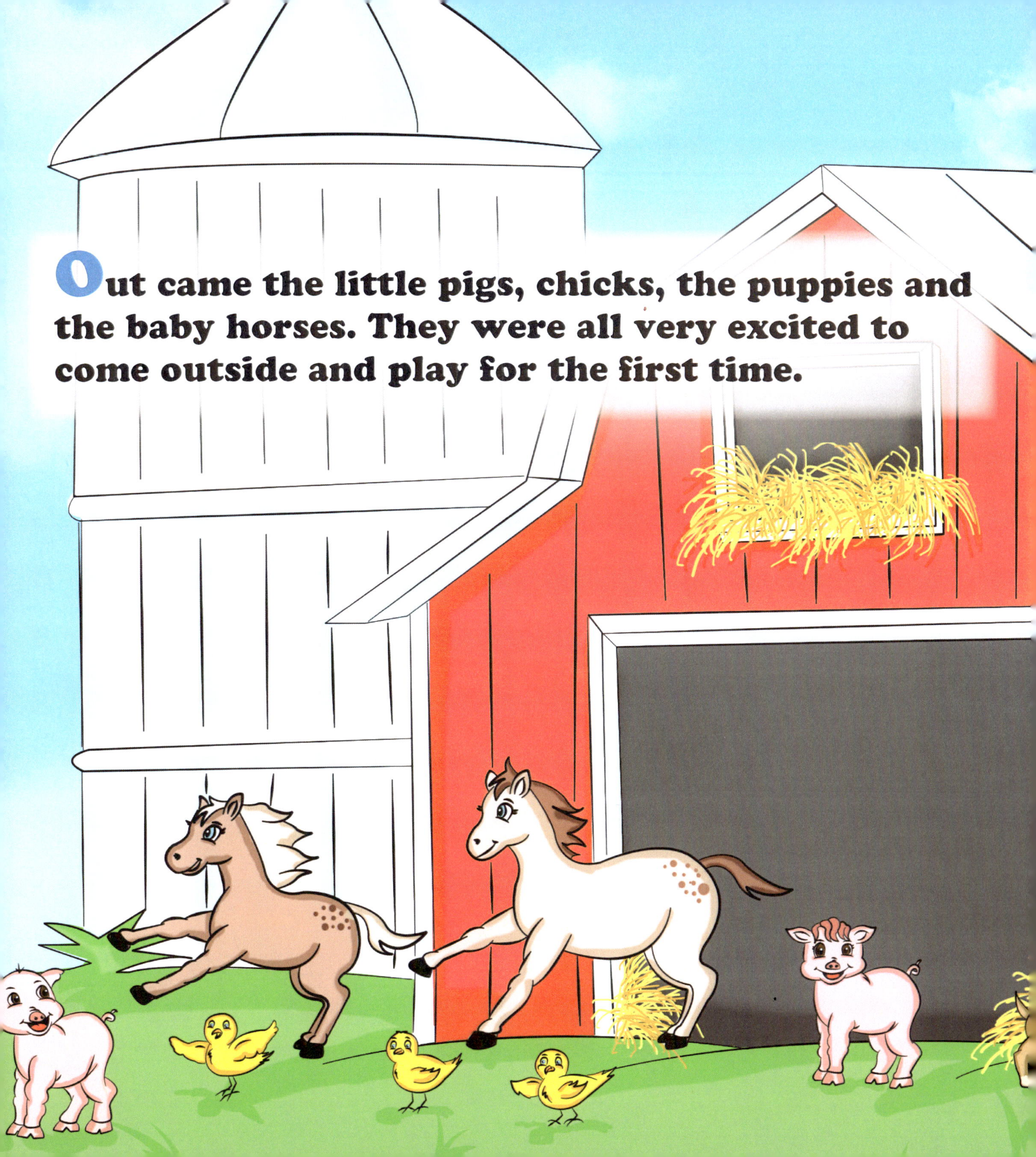

Out came the little pigs, chicks, the puppies and the baby horses. They were all very excited to come outside and play for the first time.

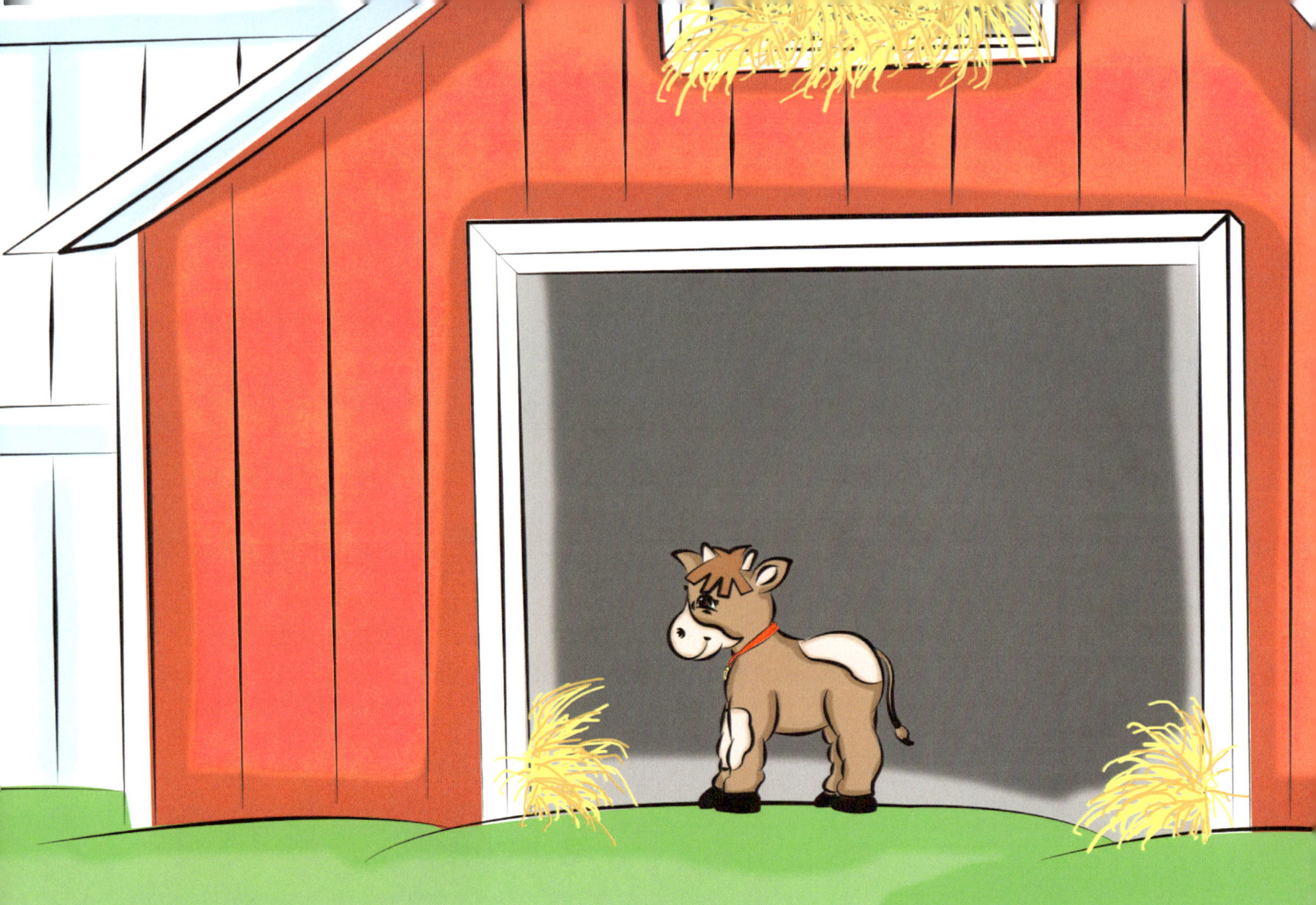

A little baby cow came out last, and looked around at all the little pigs, chicks, puppies, and horses. He could not wait to make new friends.

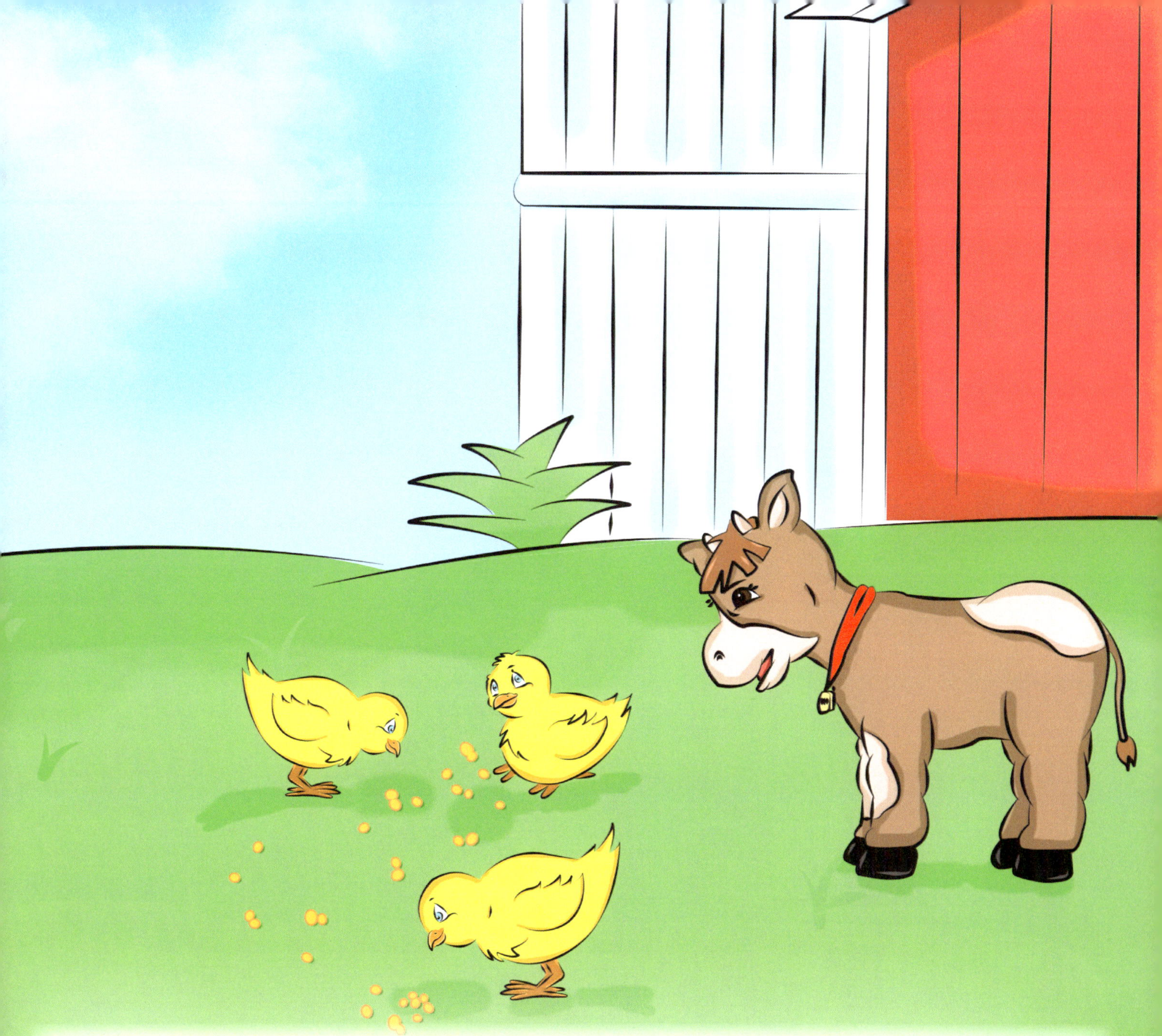

He went to the little chicks that were eating corn, and tried to join them. He asked them "How do you do that?"

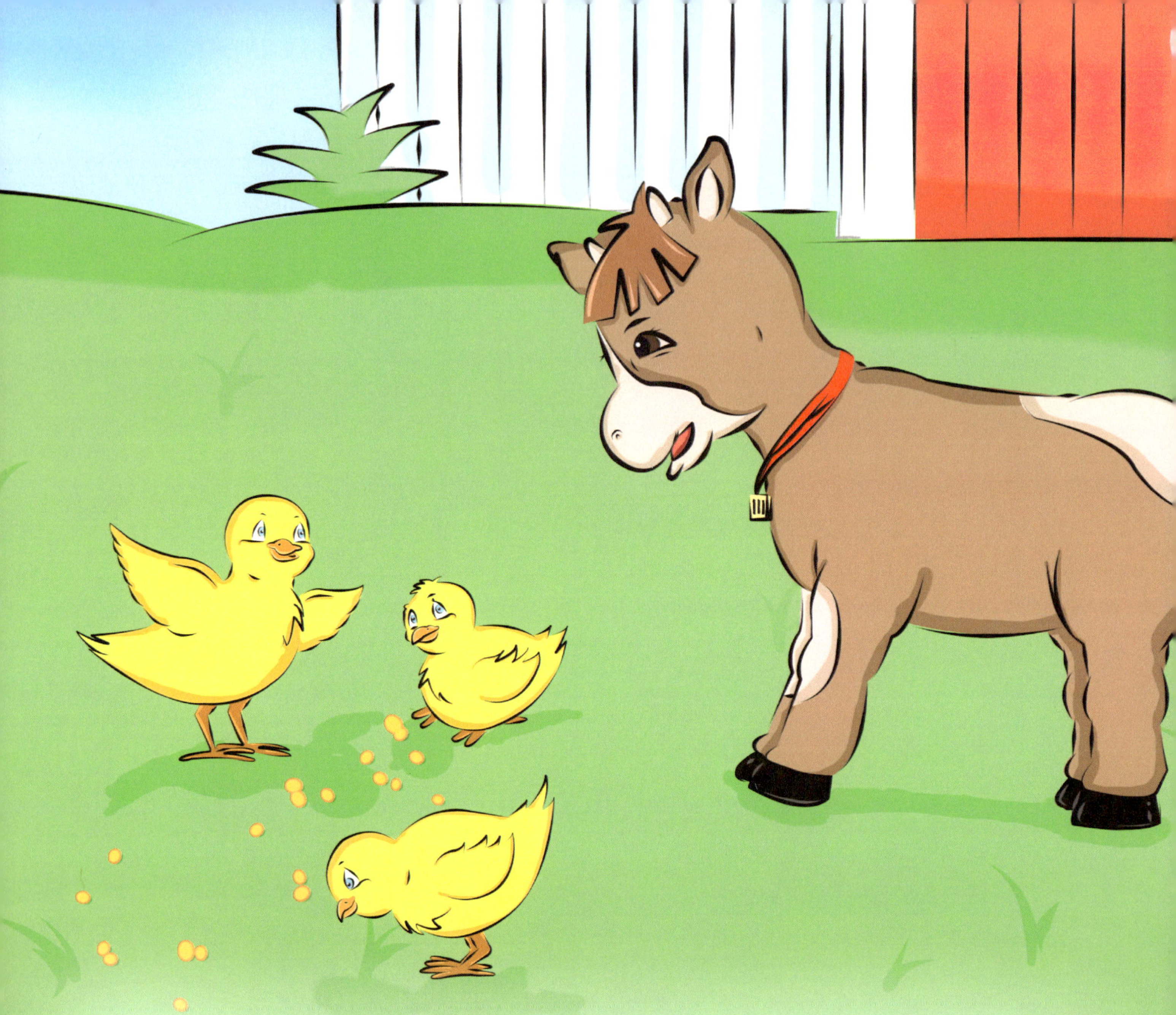

"That's easy" said the little chicks. (Not for me) thought the little baby cow. He tried to, but could not peck the corn like the little chicks.

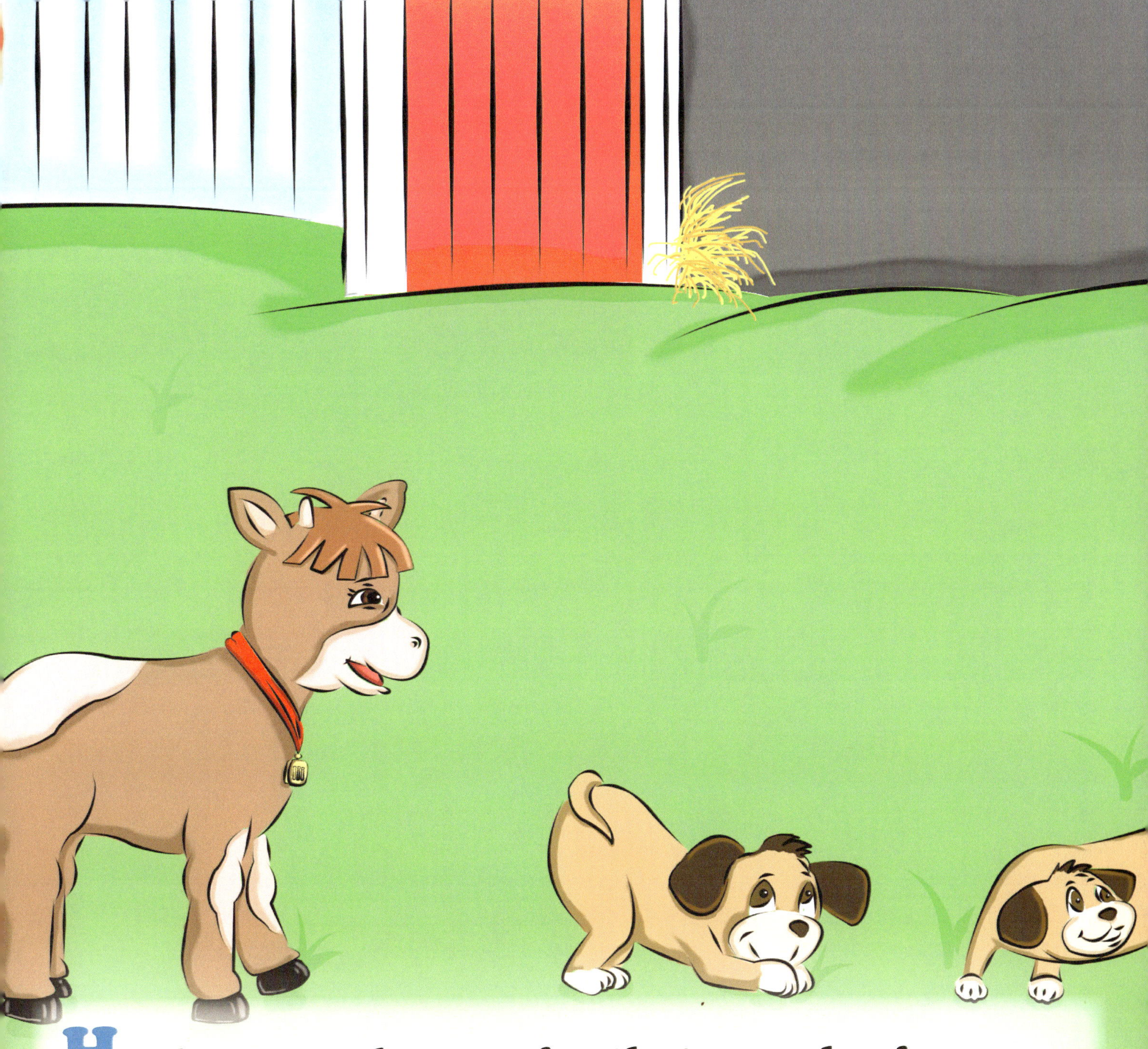

He then saw the puppies that were having so much fun chasing their own tails. The little baby cow tried too, but could not even turn around fast enough to see his own tail.

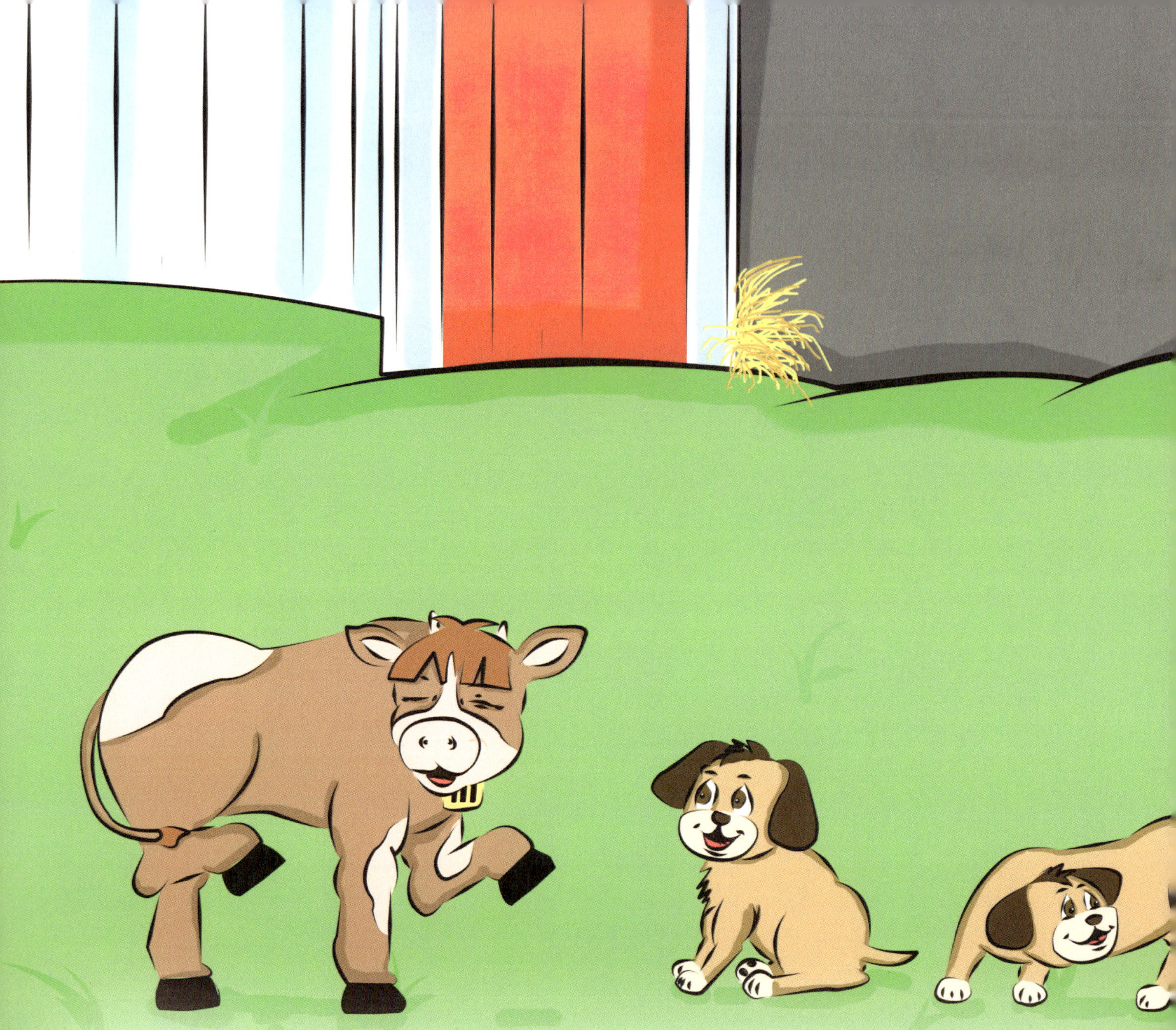

"**H**ow do you do you do that?" Asked the little cow. "That's easy" said the puppies. (Not for me) thought the little baby cow.

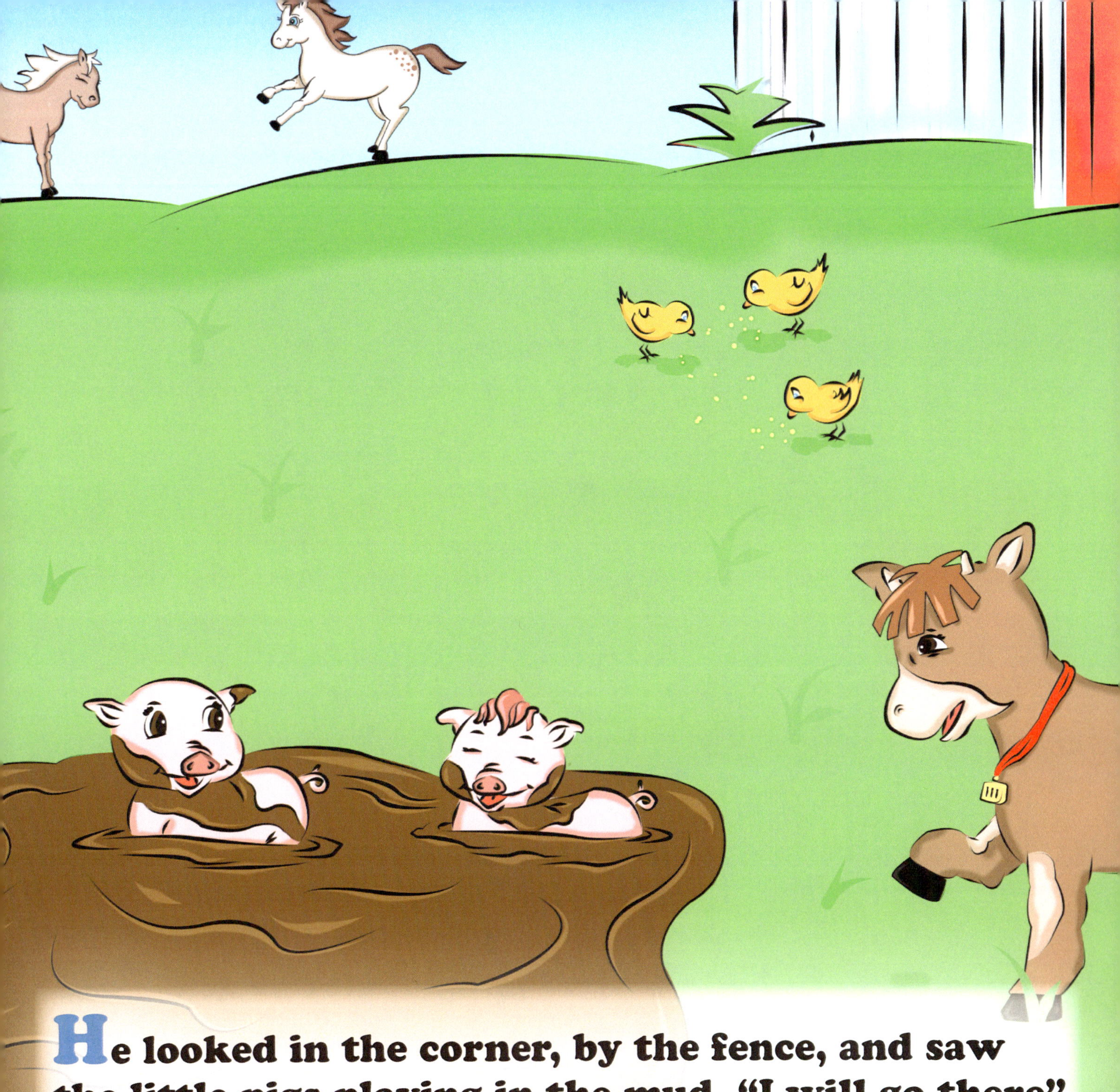

He looked in the corner, by the fence, and saw the little pigs playing in the mud. "I will go there" said the little baby cow.

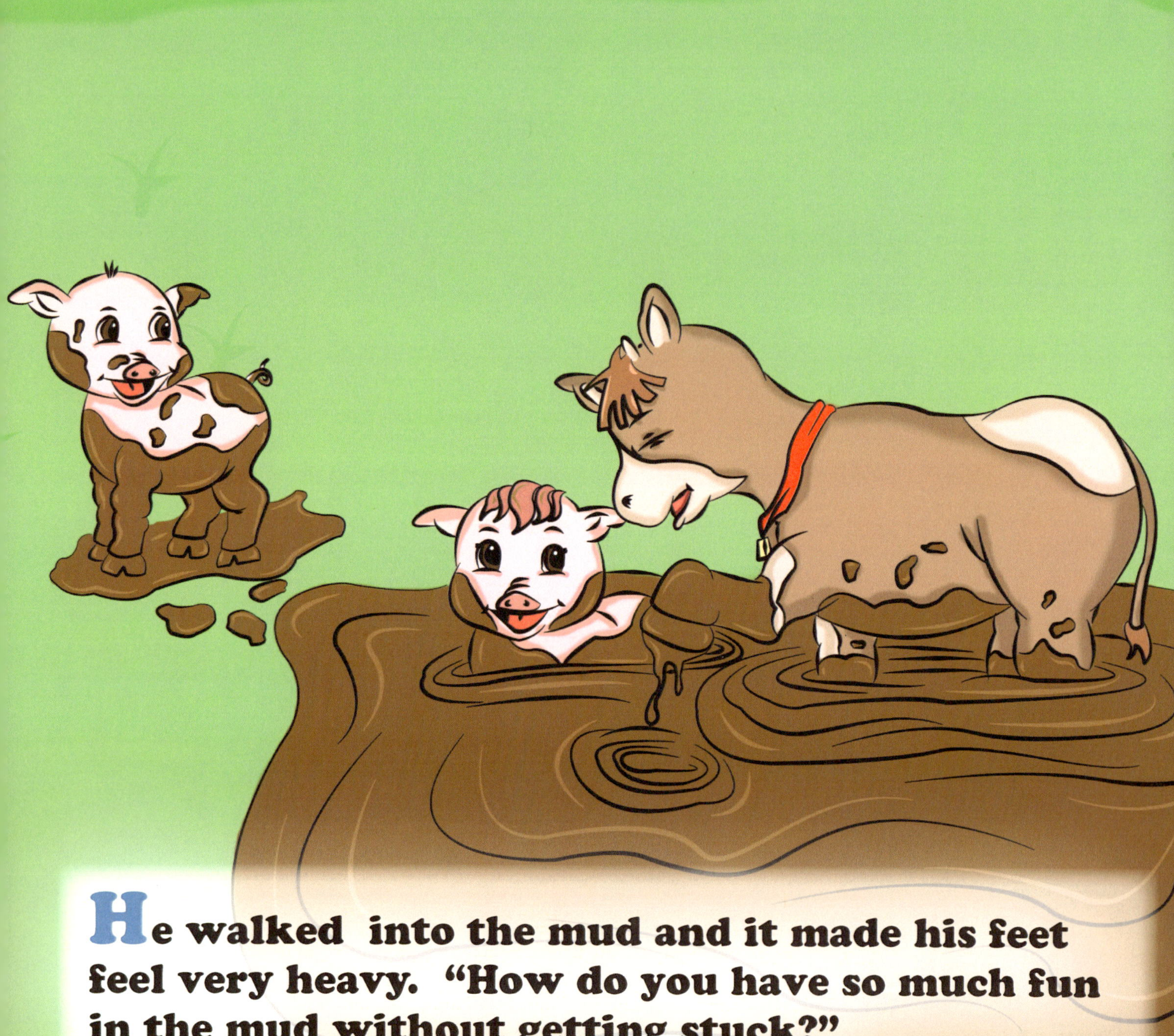

He walked into the mud and it made his feet feel very heavy. "How do you have so much fun in the mud without getting stuck?"

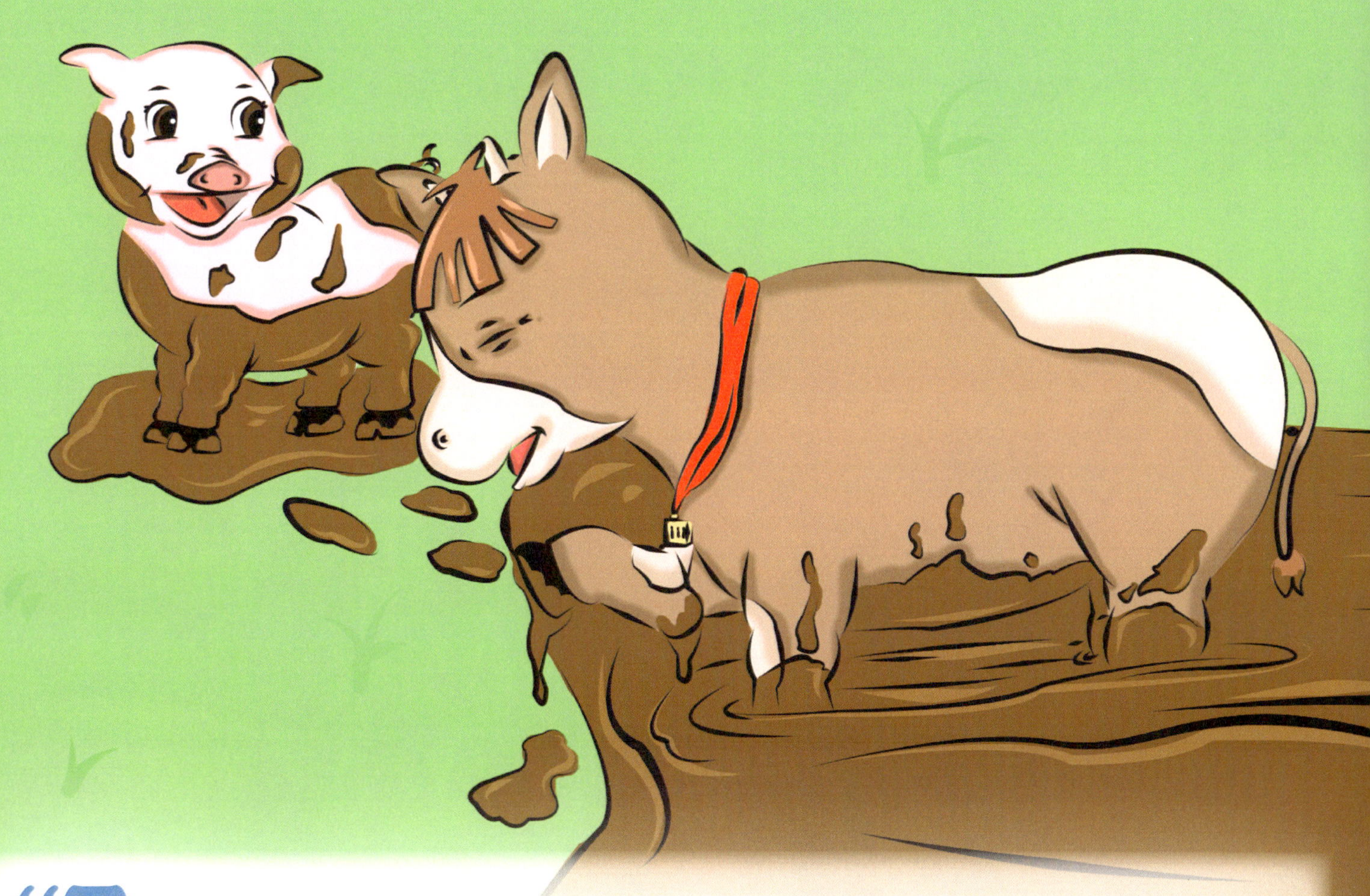

"That's easy" said the little pigs as they played, and had fun. (Not for me) Thought the little baby cow.

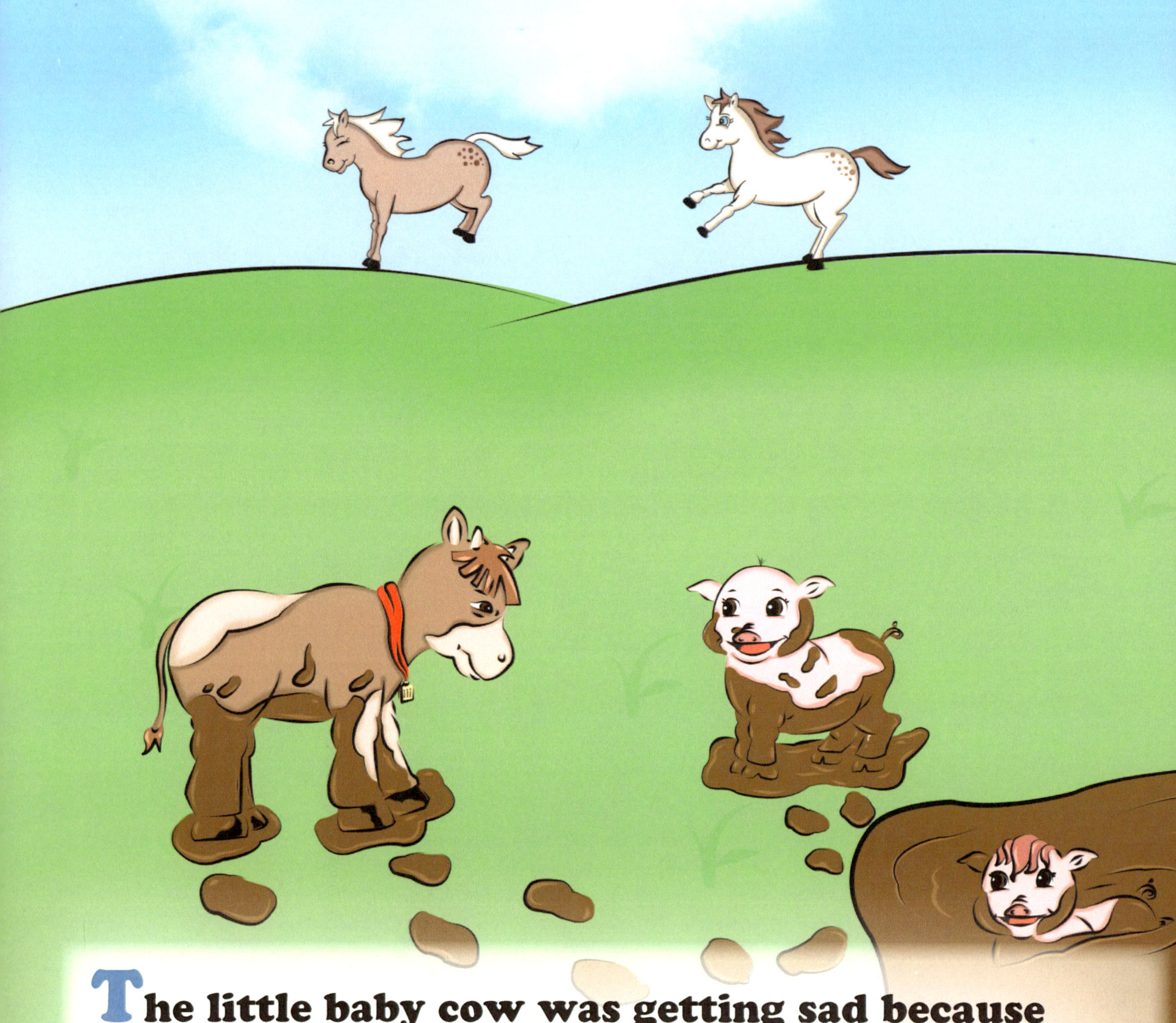

The little baby cow was getting sad because everything was easy for everyone else and not for him. He then saw the baby horses jumping and went to see them.

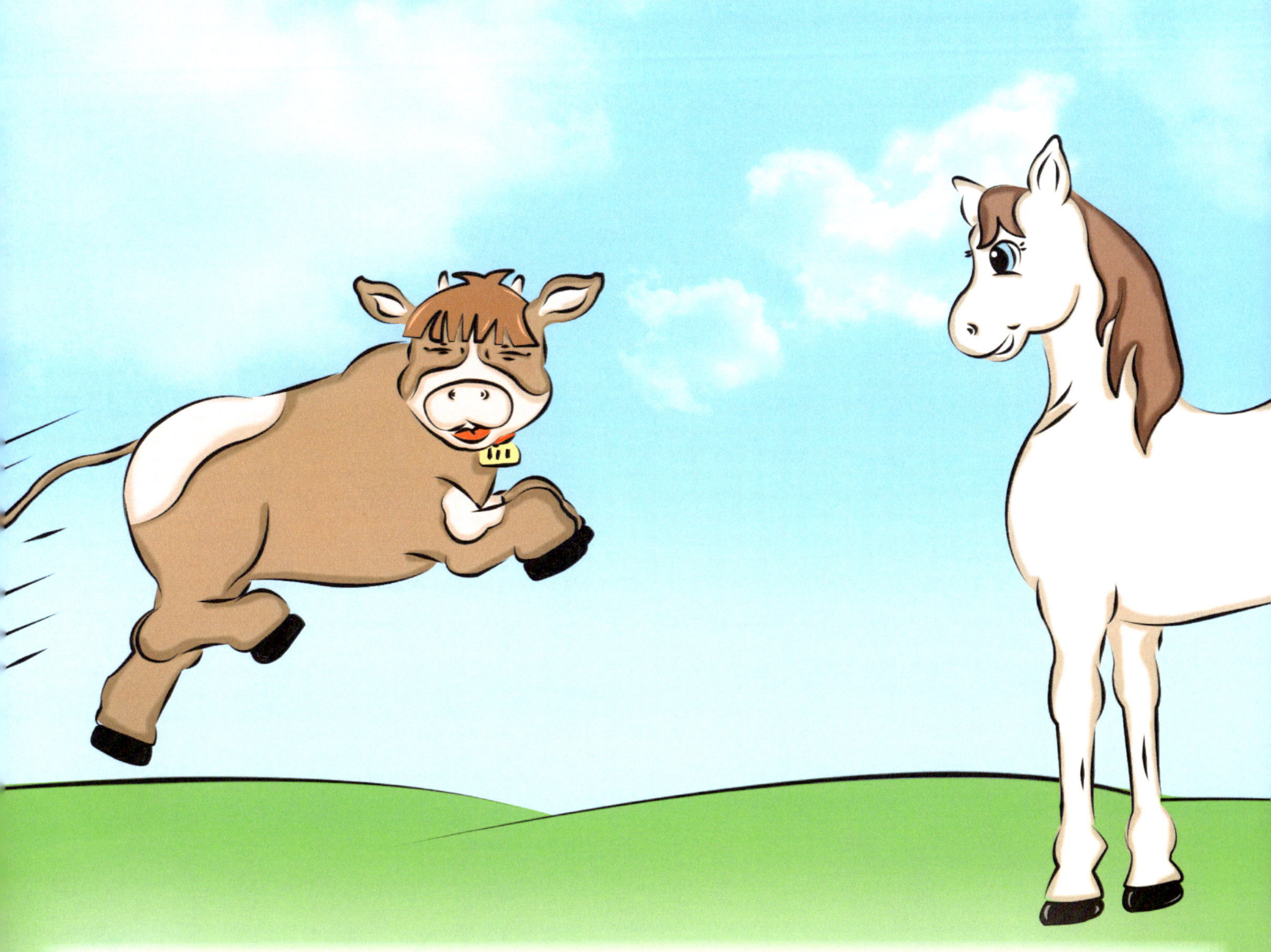

He tried to jump with the baby horses, but could not jump like them. "How do you jump like that?" asked the little baby cow.

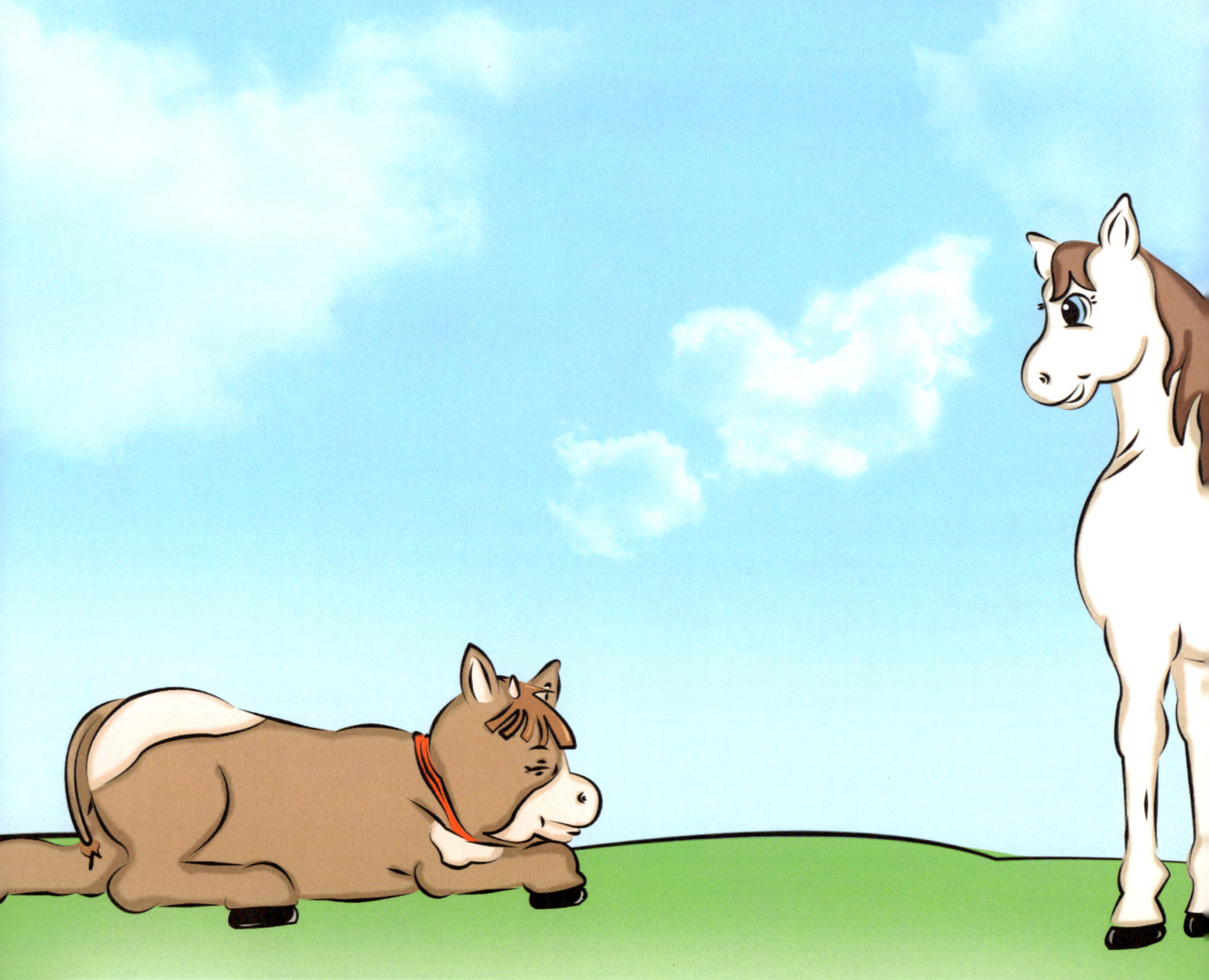

"That's easy" said the little horse's as they jumped and played. (Not for me) thought the little baby cow as he walked off.

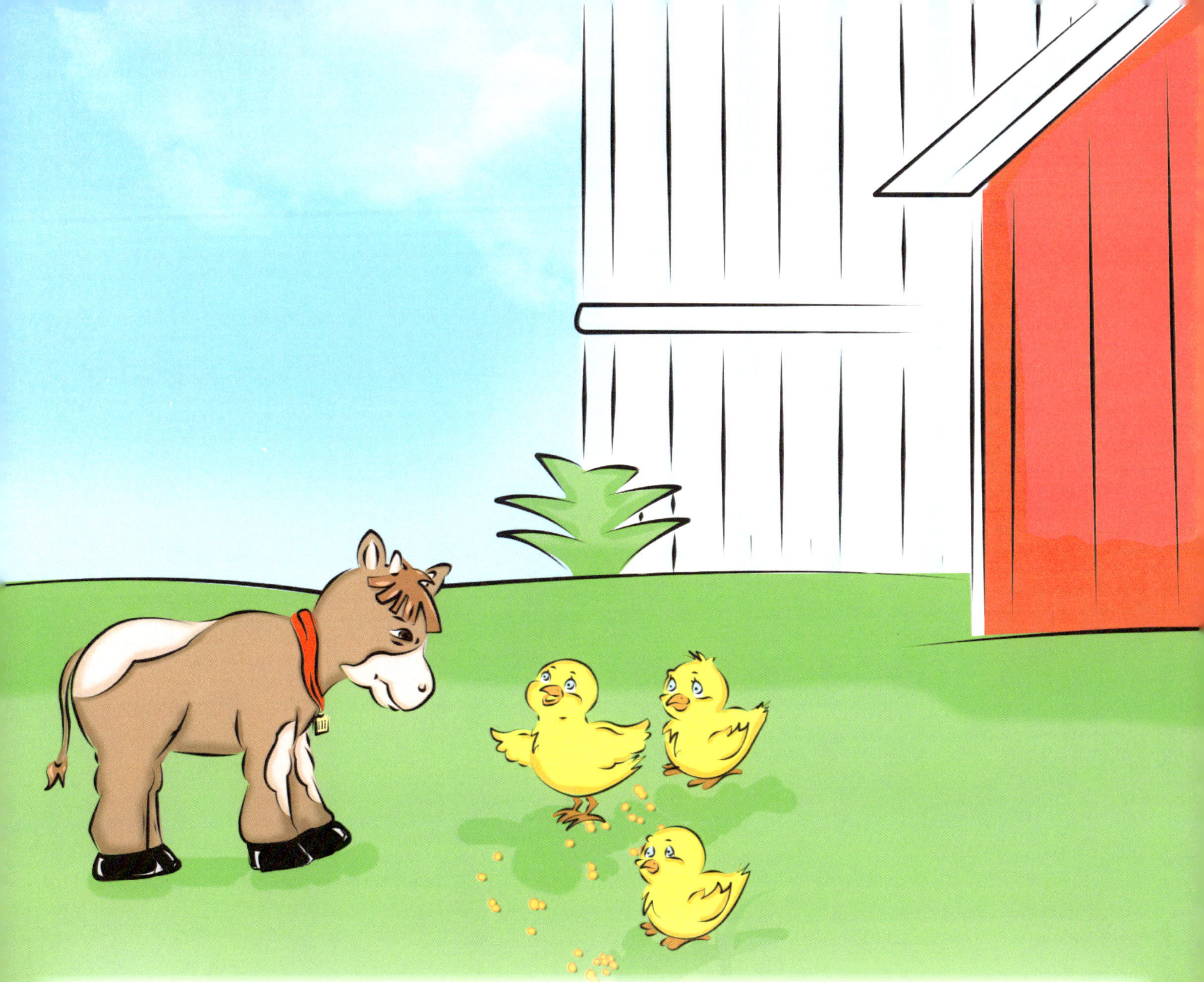

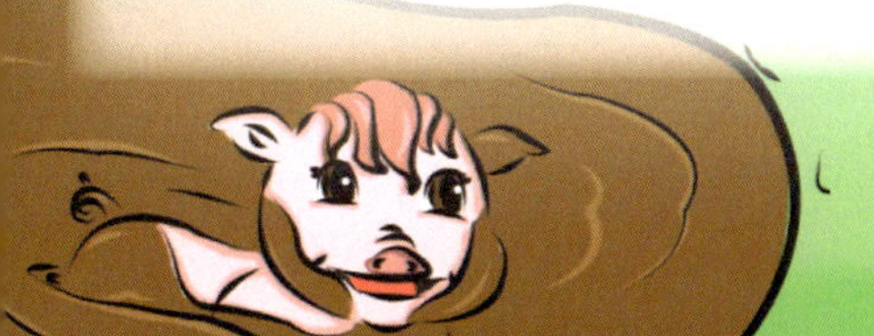

The little baby cow was so sad that everything
was easy for everybody else except him.
He began to walk back into the barn.

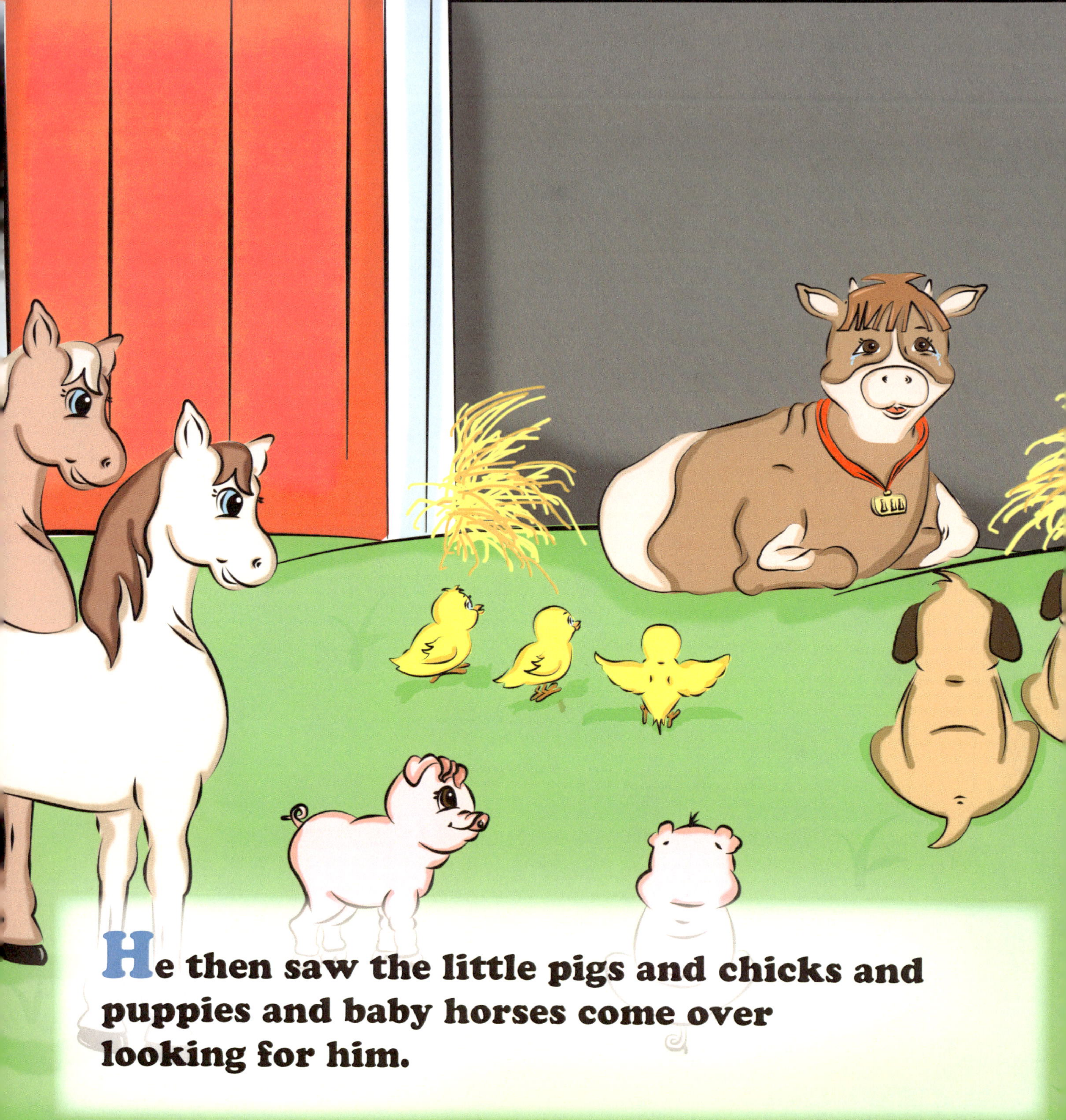

He then saw the little pigs and chicks and puppies and baby horses come over looking for him.

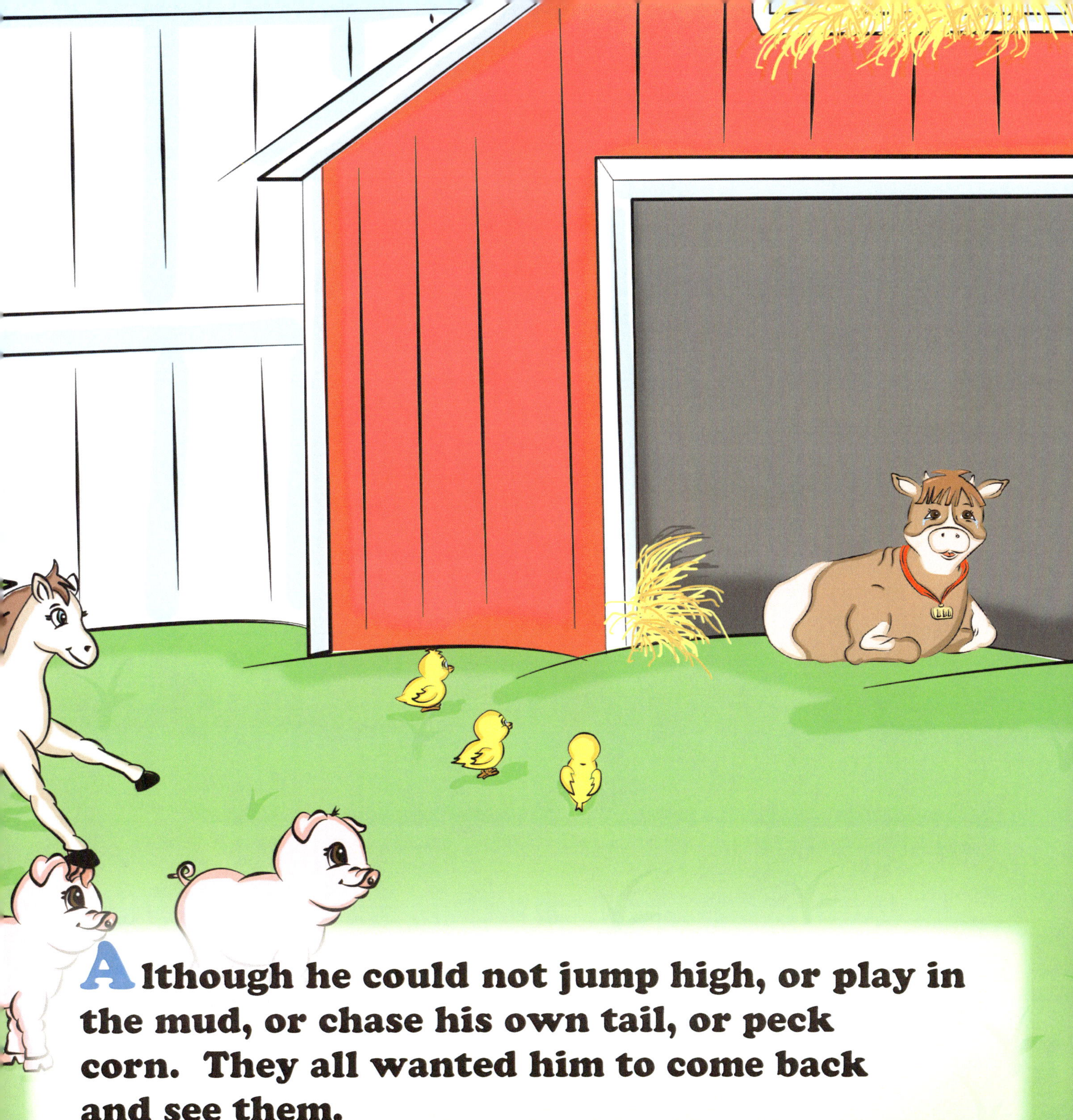

Although he could not jump high, or play in the mud, or chase his own tail, or peck corn. They all wanted him to come back and see them.

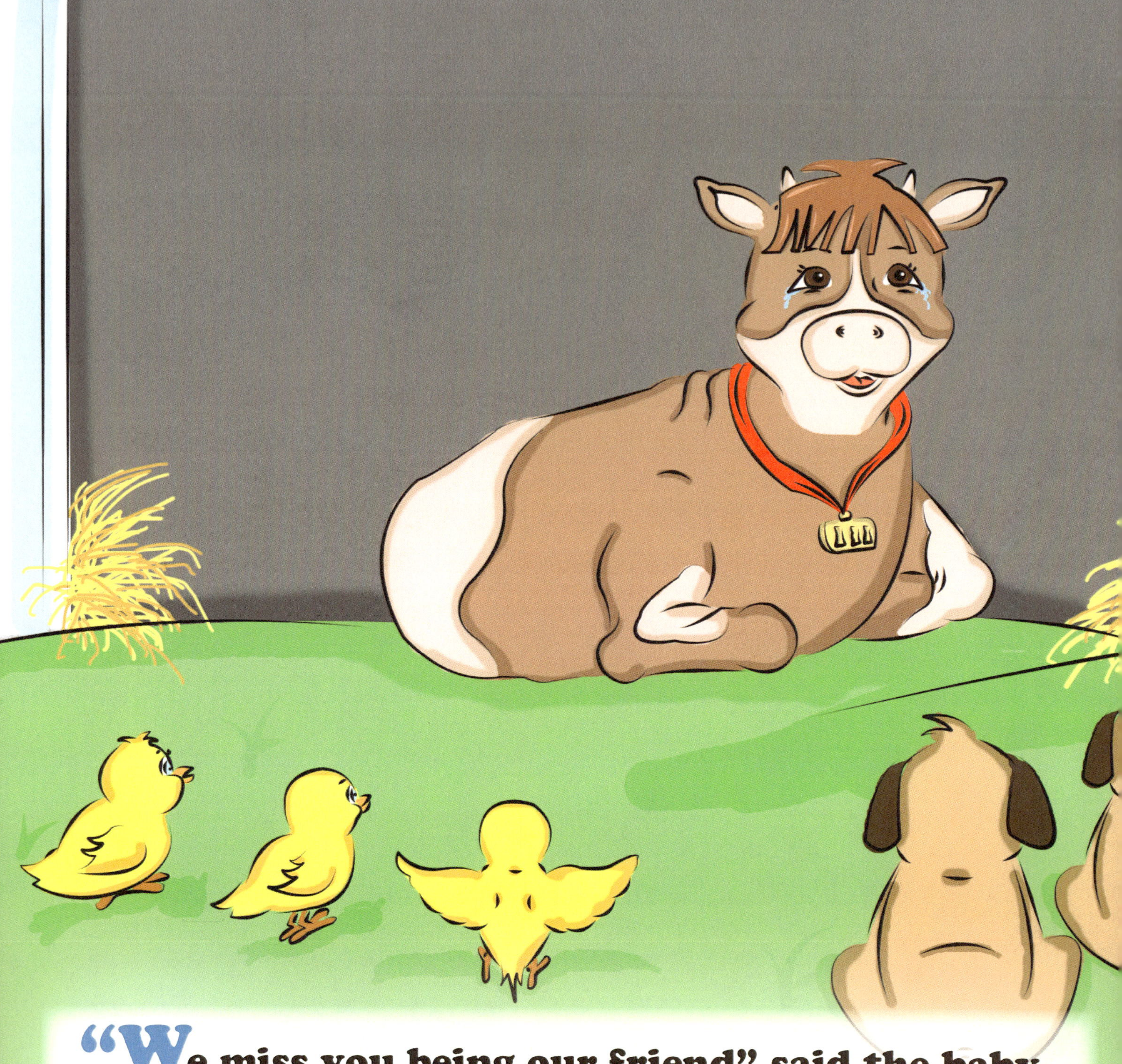

"We miss you being our friend" said the baby animals. "How did you do that?" they asked.

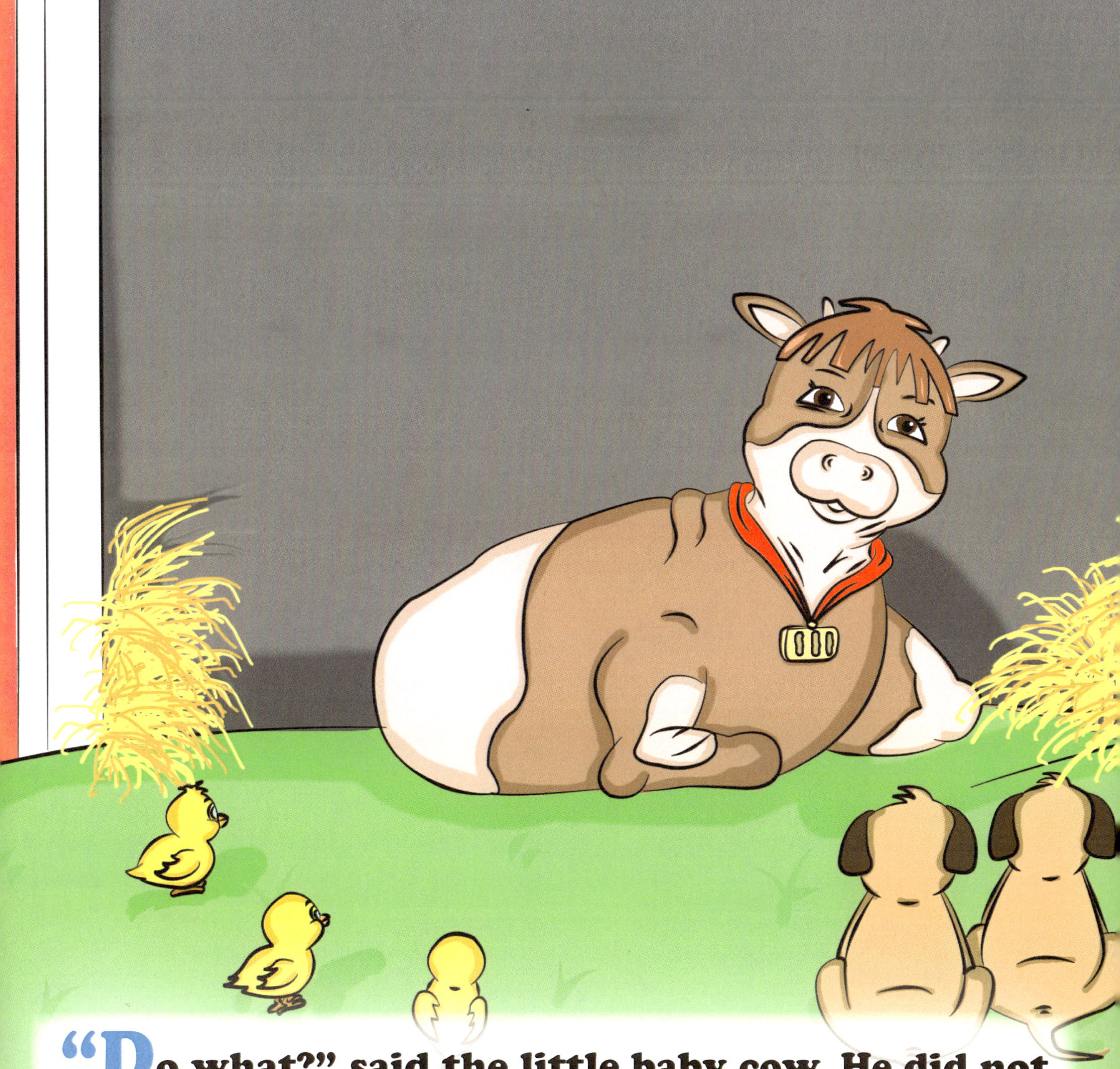

"**D**o what?" said the little baby cow. He did not know what they were asking.

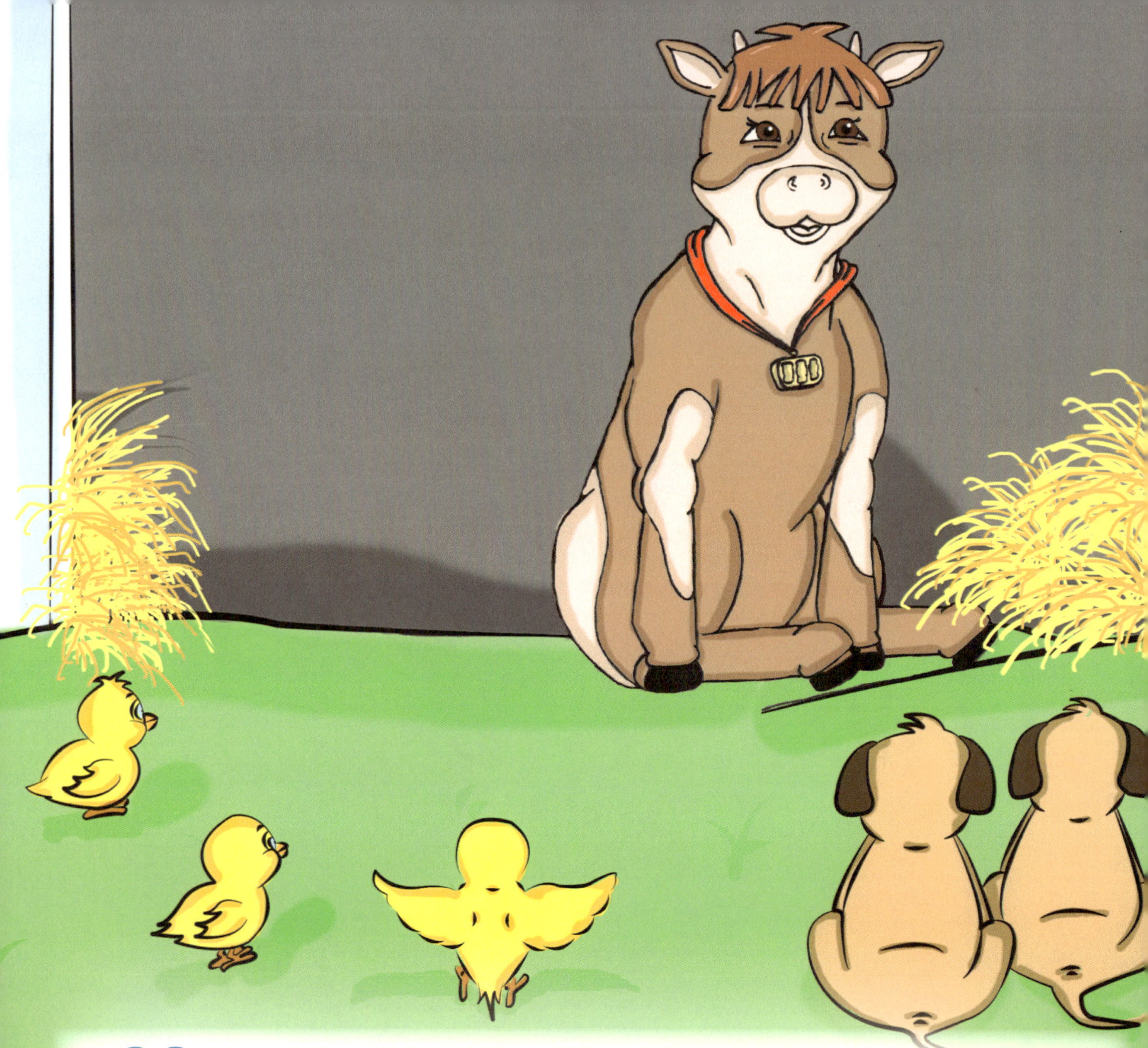

Make friends with all of us so quickly" said the baby animals.

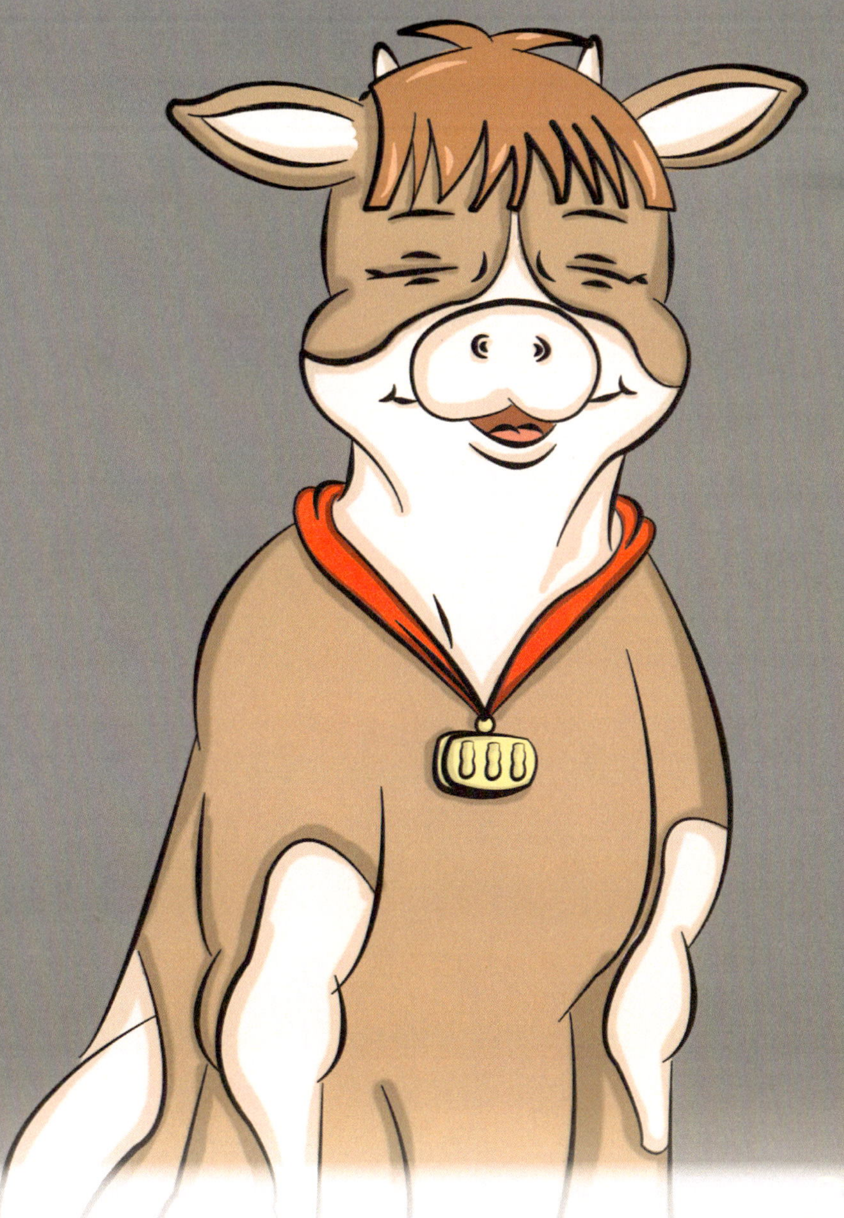

"**T**hat's easy" said the little baby cow. He was very happy because he had found what was easy for him. He played everyday with everybody and it was **EASY.**

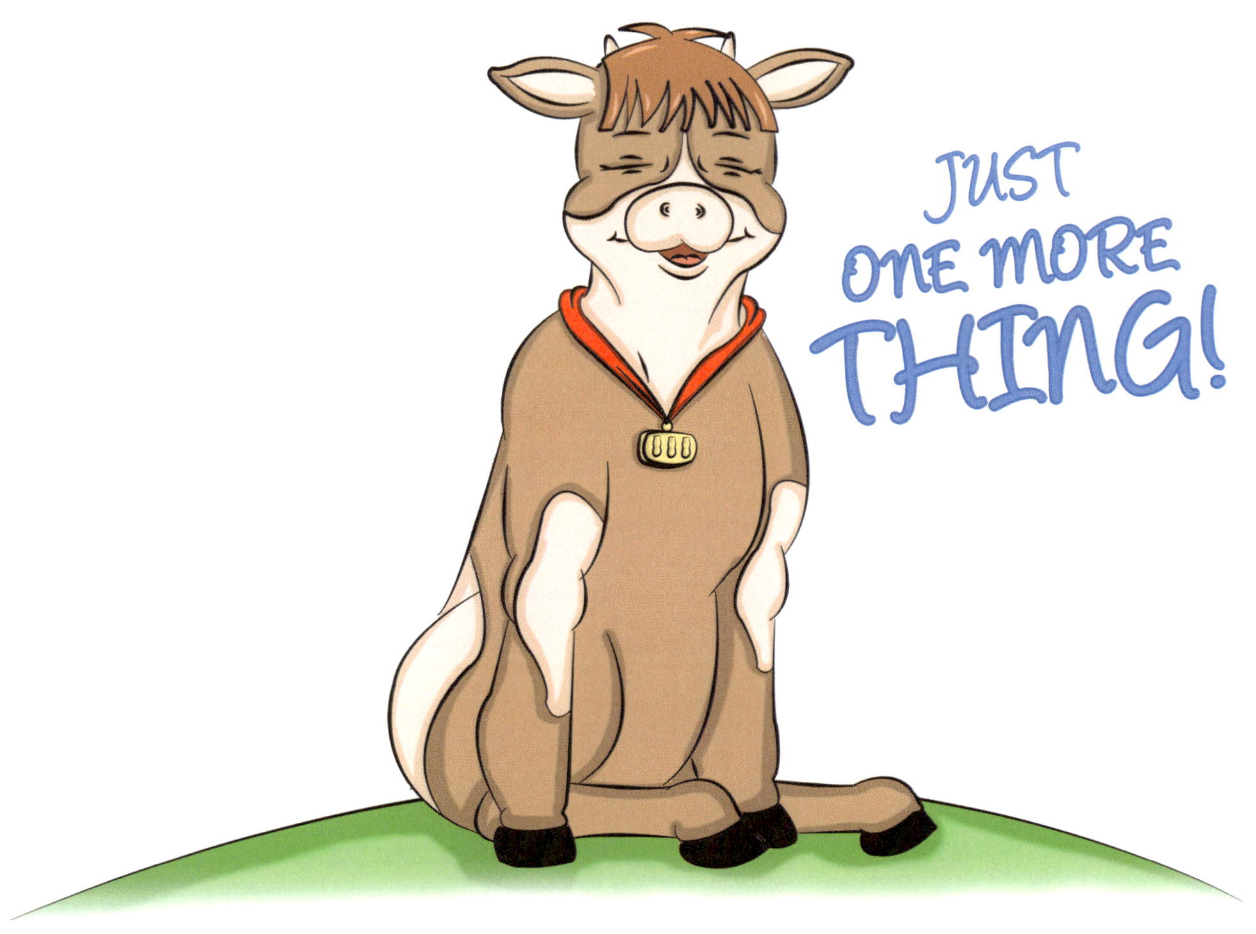

"This story is dedicated to all children with unique talents that teach and bless every life they touch"